You Have the Power!

By Zakiyyah Nelson

Illustrated by Sergio Drumond

This book is dedicated to my wonderful family and friends and also my loving husband who has supported me from the beginning. This book is also dedicated to my goddaughter Zaya. You all are my inspiration!

My dearest children you were chosen to come to the planet because you are special and you have a purpose. You have the power to change the world.

My dearest children, you have the power to cultivate the earth that was once old and transform it into a new story to be told.

My dearest children, you have the power to use your knowledge and your voice to stand for up for what is true, remember who you are because the power lives within YOU.

My dearest children, you have the power to show human beings, many things that we may not see. You have the power to open up our eyes so that we will become free.

My dearest children, you have the power to illuminate kindness to all that is and forever will be. It is your turn to create a peaceful world of perfect harmony.

My dearest children, you have the power to show us how to exist in a rainbow of love. Many blessings you bring to us from above.

My dearest children, you have the power to show gratitude for all that you are. Always remember, that you are the most beautiful and brightest star.

My dearest children, you have the power to show generosity and give from the heart. Show everyone what inside and that you are smart.

My dearest children, you have the power to create the change you want to see. It lives in you and it also lives in me.

Let's change this world together as one family.

CPSIA information can be obtained
at www.ICGtesting.com
Printed in the USA
LVHW012200271120
672813LV00011B/208